MACMILLAN READERS

BEGINNER LEVEL

MARK TWAIN

The Adventures of Huckleberry Finn

Retold by F. H. Cornish

macmillan education

Macmillan Readers is a series of engaging narrative texts designed to stimulate learners while enhancing their language skills, building literacy and boosting reading confidence. Through captivating stories and fascinating cultural themes, learners will explore a diversity of scenarios that foster vocabulary expansion, comprehension skills and a lifelong love of reading.

The right reader at every stage

Tailored to each learner's stage of language proficiency, our six levels feature text adapted to match the skill level. With controlled vocabulary and grammar, learners can read freely and immerse themselves in the story. When more challenging words are introduced, either the text will provide sufficient context to aid understanding or a full explanation will be provided in the Glossary.

Readers for all, anywhere, anytime

Macmillan Readers are perfect for shared, guided and independent reading. Whether in traditional print, immersive audio or the convenient eBook, Macmillan Readers are equally effective for in-class activities, paired discussions or solo reading at home or on the move.

Reading for pleasure, knowledge and well-being

Regular reading and reading for pleasure:

- increases reading confidence, benefiting all literacy skills, not just reading.
- reinforces and enriches vocabulary, providing a variety of contexts.
- expands general knowledge.
- supports concentration, inner reflection and well-being.

Macmillan Readers will inspire a love for reading in English while nurturing essential language skills. Unlock new worlds, expand horizons and embark on an adventure in English!

(NOTE: While the content of Macmillan Readers is evaluated for age suitability, we kindly remind parents and teachers that they are ultimately responsible for determining whether a particular book is appropriate for their child or student.)

Contents

Missouri River
Hannibal
(St Petersburg)
Illinois River
ILLINOIS
INDIANA
N
W
E
S
Jackson's
Island
East St Louis
St Louis
Ohio River
MISSOURI
KENTUCKY
Cairo
TENNESSEE
Mississippi River
Memphis
ARKANSAS
MISSISSIPPI
LOUISIANA
New Orleans
Gulf of Mexico

A Note About the Author

Samuel Langhorne Clemens was an American writer. He used the name **Mark Twain.** Samuel was born on 30th November 1835. He lived in Hannibal, in the state of Missouri. Missouri is in the centre of the United States. Hannibal is a small town on the west side of the Mississippi River.

Samuel's father was a lawyer. He was a quiet and serious man. Samuel's mother was kind and beautiful. Samuel had one brother and one sister. Samuel had many jobs. From 1853 to 1854, he worked for a printer. Samuel learnt about books and newspapers. He wrote stories for newspapers too. He was a journalist.

In 1856, Samuel was a pilot for the boats on the Mississippi River. Pilots knew the river well. They helped the captains of the boats. The captains had to guide the boats along the river. The pilots helped with this job. The Mississippi River is 3710 miles (5970 km) long. It is the longest river in the United States. It joins the sea at the city of New Orleans. New Orleans is on the Gulf of Mexico. In many places, the river is shallow – it is not deep.

At the time of this story, the large boats on the river were steamboats. The steamboats had flat bottoms and large paddle wheels at the back. A steam engine on the boat pushed the paddle wheel round. The paddle wheel pushed the water, and the boat moved forwards. A man stood at the front of the boat. He threw a long rope into the water. The rope had a heavy weight on one end. And there were marks on the rope, 3 feet (0.90 m) apart. The man looked at the rope in the water. Then he knew the depth of the water. He shouted the depth to the pilot. At some places, he shouted 'mark twain!'. This meant, 'second mark!'. At that place, the water was only 6 feet (1.80 m) deep. Samuel Clemens heard this shout many times. When he wrote stories, he took these words for his name – Mark Twain.

Mark Twain had many adventures. Later, he wrote about these adventures in his stories. From 1861 to 1865, there was a civil war in the United States. Mark Twain joined the Confederate Army. He fought for the southern states in the war. After that, he went to the western part of the country – to Nevada and California. There, he was a journalist and a gold miner. He wrote his first story in 1865.

In 1870, Mark Twain married Olivia Langdon. They lived in Hartford, Connecticut – in the east of the United States. They had three daughters.

In 1904, Mark Twain's wife died. Mark Twain died in Redding, Connecticut on 21st April 1910.

Mark Twain wrote very many stories. Some of them

are: *The Tramp Abroad* (1880), *The Prince and the Pauper* (1881), *The Adventures of Tom Sawyer* (1876), *Life on the Mississippi* (1883), *The Adventures of Huckleberry Finn* (1884) and *A Connecticut Yankee in King Arthur's Court* (1889).

A Note About This Story

Time: 1846. **Places:** The Mississippi River, St Petersburg and other towns near the river. St Petersburg is the name the writer gives for his town, Hannibal.

At the time of this story, there were many slaves in the southern part of the United States. In the eighteenth century, landowners in Europe and America had taken people from Africa. These black Africans became the slaves of the landowners – they had to work for the landowners. The landowners did not pay the slaves – they owned them. The slaves had terrible lives. Some merchants bought and sold these African slaves – they were slave traders. Sometimes, slaves ran away from their owners. They were called runaway slaves. White people often captured runaways and got rewards of money for them.

At the beginning of the nineteenth century, the governments of Europe stopped the slave trade. People in Europe did not own slaves after that. And the Government of the United States wanted to stop the slave trade too. Soon, there were no more slaves in the states in the north eastern part of the country.

But most of the landowners in the states to the south-west of the Mississippi River, and in the southern part of the country, wanted to keep their slaves. Some good landowners in these states gave their slaves freedom. After that, they were no longer slaves.

At the time of this story (1846), some of the states in the US were free states. These were the states in the north-east. There were no slaves in these states. It was not legal to have slaves in these states. And in these states, it was not legal to capture slaves from other states. Most of the southern states were slave states – people there owned many slaves. In this story, Arkansas and Missouri are slave states. And in some other states (e.g. Illinois), white people did not own slaves, but they captured runaways from slave states. It was legal to do this. The white people took the runaways back to their owners and got rewards for them.

Note: Cairo = 'kaɪrəʊ New Orleans = njuː 'ɔːliːənz
Arkansas = 'ɑːkənsɔː Missouri = mɪz'ʊəri
Mississippi = mɪsɪ'sɪpi St Louis = seɪnt 'luːɪs
(St = Saint, e.g. St Petersburg)

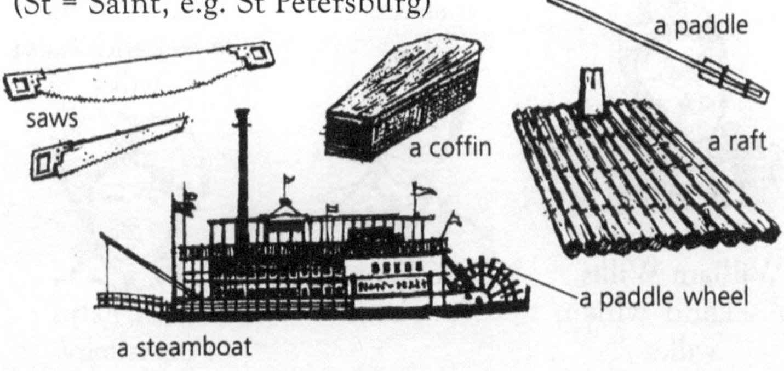

The People in This Story

Huckleberry Finn
'hʌklberi fɪn

Mr Finn
'mɪstə fɪn

Jim
dʒɪm

Mrs Douglas
'mɪsɪz 'dʌgləs

Miss Watson
mɪs wɒtsən

The Duke

The King

The three sisters

The Second Harvey Wilks
ðə 'sekənd 'hɑːvi wɪlks

The Second William Wilks
ðə 'sekənd 'wiljəm wɪlks

Tom Sawyer
tɒm 'sɔːjə

Mrs Phelps
'mɪsɪz felps

1

Writers Don't Know Everything!

My name is Huckleberry Finn. My friends call me Huck. I am fourteen years old.

Have you heard about me? Have you read about me and my friend, Tom Sawyer? Mr Twain wrote a book about us. The book was about both of us, but Mr Twain called it *The Adventures of Tom Sawyer*. The stories in that book are true. But Mr Twain didn't tell you everything about us. He didn't know everything about us. He was a writer, not a boy. Writers don't know everything about boys!

Now *I'm* going to tell you some more of my story. But first, I'm going to remind you about myself.

I was born in St Petersburg, in the state of Missouri. St Petersburg is on the western shore of the Mississippi River. My mother died a long time ago. After that, my father left the town and I lived alone.

Tom Sawyer's mother was dead too. But Tom lived with his aunt – Aunt Polly. I didn't have any aunts. I lived alone for many years. In the summer, I slept in the fields near the river. In the winter, I slept in barns on the farms near the town. I didn't go to school and I didn't learn lessons. I didn't go to church and I didn't say prayers. I didn't wash my face and I didn't comb my hair. My life was good!

I didn't have any aunts. I didn't have any brothers or sisters. But I had many friends.

Most of the boys in St Petersburg were my friends. But their mothers and fathers weren't my friends! Their mothers and fathers didn't want me to come to their houses. They didn't want me to talk to their children. Why? Because their children didn't like going to school. And their children didn't like going to church. All my friends wanted to be me! Their parents didn't like that.

What about my father? I didn't see him very often. Sometimes he came to St Petersburg. But he was a bad man. He was always drunk. He often hit me and he stole things from me. I was afraid of him.

Two years ago, in 1844, Tom Sawyer and I had an adventure. There were two bad men in our town. They had stolen some money and they had hidden it. They wanted to attack an old widow. One of the bad men hated this widow – Mrs Douglas. Her husband was dead. He had been a judge. Some years before, he had sent this man to prison. The man wanted to hurt Mrs Douglas. He and his friend wanted to get into her house. They wanted to cut her face and her ears.

Tom and I found out about the men's plan. And Tom and I told Judge Thatcher about it. I was angry about those men. I liked Mrs Douglas. She was kind to me. She sometimes gave me food and clothes.

Judge Thatcher and some other men went to Mrs Douglas' house. They caught one of the bad men. The other man escaped. He hid in a cave in the side of a hill. But he soon died there. Tom Sawyer knew about the man's hiding place. He told Judge Thatcher about it. The men from the town found the stolen money in the cave.

After that, everybody in St Petersburg was pleased with Tom. And they were pleased with me too. My friends' parents smiled at me. They spoke to me. They invited me to their houses! And Judge Thatcher gave the money from the cave to Tom and me. We each had six thousand dollars! Judge Thatcher took care of it for us. Every week he gave us five dollars.

One day, Mrs Douglas found me in a barn. She took me to her house.

'This is your home now, Huckleberry,' the widow said. 'You saved me from those bad men. Now I'm going to take care of you. You're going to live here with me. You'll sleep in a soft bed every night. And you'll wear clean clothes.'

'You'll go to school every day, except Sundays,' Mrs Douglas said. 'You'll learn about reading and writing. You'll wash your face every morning and you'll comb your hair every day. And on Sundays, we will go to church. You'll be happy with me, Huckleberry!'

But I wasn't happy. I liked Mrs Douglas. I tried to please her. But I don't like beds. I don't like clean clothes and I don't like washing my face.

And there was another problem. Mrs Douglas had a sister. Her name was Miss Watson. She lived in Mrs Douglas' house too.

Miss Watson owned a slave – an old black man. His name was Jim.

I liked Jim. He was kind to me. But I didn't like his owner and she didn't like me. Mrs Douglas wanted me to be clean. That was bad! But her sister wanted me to be good. That was worse!

'You must read the Bible every day,' Miss Watson said to me. 'And you must be a better person.'

But I didn't *want* to be a better person. I wanted to be happy!

At the end of his book about Tom and me, Mr Twain wrote this –

> **Huck did not want to stay in St Petersburg for ever. One day, he got into a small boat and he went south. He travelled down the Mississippi River. But that is another story!**

This book is that other story. Mr Twain didn't know everything about me. I did leave St Petersburg. I wasn't happy in Mrs Douglas' house. That's true. But that wasn't the reason for my journey. The reason was this – my father came back to St Petersburg!

2

The Cabin in the Forest

I told you the truth. I wasn't happy with Mrs Douglas and Miss Watson. I didn't like going to school and I didn't like reading the Bible. School was boring. The Bible was boring. Everything in my life was boring! But one evening, my father came back to St Petersburg. After that, I wanted a boring life again!

That evening, I went to my bedroom at nine o'clock. My father was in my room. He was waiting for me. He had climbed into the room through a window. His hair was long and his clothes were dirty. He was holding a bottle of whisky. He was drunk.

I wanted to call Mrs Douglas, but my father put his hand over my mouth.

'Be quiet!' he said. 'Listen to me! You are a bad son! I've heard about you. You go to school every day! You're learning about reading and writing! Why? I didn't go to school. I can't read and write! Why do you want to read and write?'

'You're my son,' my father said. He hit me. 'But you've never been a good son to me. That is going to change now. You're going to be a good son! I've heard about your money. You've got $6000. It's my money now. I want it. Get it for me! Get it tomorrow! Do you understand me?'

'I understand you,' I said. 'But I'm not going to give my money to you!'

Then my father hit me again. 'Get me the money tomorrow,' he said. 'And don't tell anybody about my visit.'

He climbed quickly out of the window. He disappeared into the darkness of the night.

The next day, my father spoke to Judge Thatcher. Mrs Douglas told me about it in the evening.

'Give me the $6000,' my father said to the judge. 'It's my money now!'

'No! It isn't your money!' Judge Thatcher replied. 'It's Huckleberry's money. And I'm going to take care of it for him!'

The next day, my father spoke to a lawyer about the money. Mrs Douglas found out about that too.

'I want to get Huck's money from Judge Thatcher,' my father told the lawyer. 'How shall I do it?'

'You must ask for the money in a law court,' the lawyer said. 'You must tell another judge about the money. You love your son and you want him to live with you. You must tell the judge that. The judge will listen to you. But he will listen to Judge Thatcher too. He will listen to both of you. Then he will make a decision.'

'But Judge Thatcher is a clever man,' the lawyer said. 'He knows about law courts. He knows the other judges. A judge will listen to your story but you will have to wait for many weeks. Will the judge give the money to you? I don't know. Your son doesn't live with you now. That will be a problem for you.'

The next morning, I started to walk to school. But my father was waiting for me near Mrs Douglas' house. He hit me. Then he held my arm.

'You must come with me!' he shouted. 'You're going

to live with me now!'

My father took me to an old wooden cabin. This small house was near the Mississippi River, a few miles from the town. There were tall trees around the cabin. Nobody knew about it and nobody went there. The cabin was a secret place. It became our home.

My father went out every day, but he locked me in the cabin. I was lonely and unhappy. I wanted to see Tom Sawyer. I wanted to see Mrs Douglas. I wanted to see Miss Watson!

The cabin was old, but it was very strong. Somebody had built it from big logs of wood. The wooden door was very strong too, and there was a strong lock on the door.

You are asking yourself a question. What did my father do every day? This is the answer – he sold logs.

At that time of year, there were many big logs in the river. They were floating down the river from the north. In the north of the country, people cut down big trees near the river. They cut them down with saws, and then they cut the trees into logs. They tied many logs together with ropes – they made the logs into large rafts.

Men travelled on these rafts. They travelled south, down the great Mississippi River. The rafts floated down the river and the men lived on the rafts. Then one day, they untied the logs. They sold the logs to people in the towns and cities next to the river.

The logs of the rafts were tied together with ropes. But sometimes the ropes broke. Then the rafts broke. The men swam to the shore and the logs floated on down the river.

Every day, my father went to the shore of the river and he looked for good, big logs. Then he paddled out to them in an old canoe. He pulled the logs to St Petersburg and he sold them there. He bought food for us with the money. And he bought whisky for himself.

Every evening, he was very drunk. And every evening he hit me. He shouted at me.

'You're not my son! You're the Spirit of Death!' he shouted one evening. 'You want to kill me. But I'm going to kill *you!*'

Every day, my father was worse. Every day I was more afraid. 'He will kill me soon,' I thought. I had to escape from the cabin!

One morning, I was digging in the earth in a corner of the cabin. Suddenly, I found an old saw. It wasn't big and it wasn't sharp. But I looked at it for a few moments and then I started to think about my escape. There was a cupboard in the cabin, next to the wall. I pulled the cupboard away from the wall. Then I started to cut the cabin wall with the saw. All day, I cut one of the logs near the ground. By the evening, I had cut through the log. Then my father came back to the cabin. I heard him coming and I pushed the cupboard in front of the cut log.

A moment later, my father came in. He was very angry. He hadn't got any money and he hadn't got any whisky. He hit me very hard.

The next morning, my father went out very early. I pulled the cupboard away from the wall and I started to cut the log in a second place. I made the new cut two feet from the first cut.

In the afternoon, I finished cutting the log. I lifted the piece of wood out of the wall carefully, and I crawled through the hole.

I ran quickly to the river. Soon, I found an old canoe. A few minutes later, I was paddling the canoe towards Jackson's Island.

3

Two Runaways

Jackson's Island was in the Mississippi River, about three miles south of St Petersburg. Mr Twain wrote about it in his book. Two years ago, Tom and I, and our friend Joe Harper, lived there for a few days. We wanted to be pirates. But after a few days, we had to return to the town. This time, I didn't want to be a pirate. And I didn't want to return to the town! There were good hiding places on the island. I had escaped from my father and I wanted to hide on the island till the next night. Then I wanted to travel down the river. I wanted to travel a long way from St Petersburg.

I got to the island and I hid my canoe under some trees. I was hungry, but I didn't have any food. I slept for a few hours.

In the evening, I woke up. Suddenly, I was frightened. It was dark and there was a smell of cooking. Somebody was cooking food nearby! I saw a light through the trees. It was the light from a fire. Had my father come to the island? Was he searching for me?

I walked very carefully towards the fire. Then I wasn't frightened any more. There *was* somebody else on Jackson's Island. But it wasn't my father. It was Jim, Miss Watson's slave. Jim was my friend.

I called to him quietly.

'Jim, what are you doing here?' I said.

Jim looked round suddenly. He was more frightened than I was.

'Huck!' he said. 'Huck, please don't tell anybody about me. I'm a runaway.'

'Have you run away from Miss Watson, Jim?' I asked. 'Why? She reads the Bible all day, but she's not a *bad* person.'

'She's going to sell me, Huck,' Jim replied. 'She's going to sell me to a slave trader from New Orleans. I heard them talking about me this morning. The man said, "I'll give you $800 for your slave!" But I don't want to go to New Orleans, Huck. The slaves there have terrible lives.'

'What did you do, Jim?' I asked him.

'I waited till this evening,' said Jim. Then I took some food from the kitchen and I ran away. I found a canoe and I came here. Tomorrow, the white men from the town will search for me. Please don't tell them about my hiding place, Huck.'

'Don't worry, Jim,' I said. 'I'm not going to return to St Petersburg.' Then I told Jim about my father.

'I'm sorry about your trouble, Huck,' he said. 'Sit down and eat some of this food.'

I liked Jim. He was a good man. He always told the truth and he trusted people. People often told him lies, but he always believed them. He was very kind. I wanted to stay with him for a few days.

'Jim, we're *both* runaways,' I said. 'But where shall we go?'

'We must go south, down the river, Huck,' said Jim. 'I've run away and now Miss Watson won't get the $800 from the slave trader. She'll try to find me. She'll pay a reward for me. White men will search for me on the Missouri shore and white men will search for me on the Illinois shore. We mustn't travel on the land. We must make a raft, Huck. We must travel down the river and we must live on the river. But we must travel in the dark and we must hide during the daylight.'

'But where shall we go?' I asked him again.

'In some of the states in this country, people don't own slaves, Huck,' Jim answered. 'I want to go to one of those states – the free states.'

I thought about Jim's words for a minute.

'But most of those free states are in the north of the country, Jim,' I said. 'Why do you want to go south, down the river?'

'The Mississippi is very strong, Huck,' Jim replied. 'We *have* to go south. The current will take us to the south. We'll float down the Mississippi – we won't have to paddle the raft. But we can't go north on the river. We aren't strong enough. The river current is stronger than we are!'

'We'll go south, Huck,' Jim said. 'And in a few days, we'll get to Cairo, on the eastern shore. The Ohio River joins the Mississippi there. Then I'll get on a steamboat. The boats go up the Ohio River from Cairo. They go to the free states.'

I agreed with Jim's plan.

'We'll build a raft tomorrow, Jim,' I said.

We didn't have to build a raft. The next morning, we saw one floating in the river. Nobody was on it. We paddled out to it in one of the canoes and we pulled it to the island. It was a good, strong raft – about sixteen feet long and twelve feet wide. Quickly, we built a small wooden hut on it. We hid the raft under the trees with Jim's canoe. Then we found a long wooden pole.

'We'll steer the raft with this pole, Jim,' I said. 'We'll start our journey tonight.'

But we could not start travelling that night. In the afternoon, the river started to flood!

There had been bad rainstorms in the north of the country. There was a lot of water in the river. That afternoon, the water rose higher and higher. The river was moving very fast. Soon, it flooded both shores and it started to flood Jackson's Island too. We had to move to a high place in the middle of the island.

The next morning, the river was still moving fast. It had flooded the shores and it had destroyed people's property. Parts of buildings and parts of broken boats were floating in the water. Jim and I sat quietly and we looked sadly at all these broken things. Then suddenly, we saw a little house floating down the river! It wasn't a part of a building. It was a complete house!

'I want to look inside that house, Huck,' Jim said.

Quickly, we paddled the canoe out to the house, and Jim climbed onto the building. I stayed in the canoe and held on to the floating house. Jim got into it through a window.

After a few minutes, Jim came out of the window.

'I've found some food and money, Huck,' he said.

'I want to go in there too, Jim,' I said.

'No, Huck!' Jim said quickly. 'Don't go in there. There is a dead man in there. Somebody has shot him!'

'I've seen many dead people, Jim,' I said.

Suddenly, there were tears in Jim's eyes.

'Please, Huck,' he said. 'Listen to me. You mustn't go in there. Please trust me.'

By the end of the afternoon, the river was moving more slowly. Soon, the sky began to get dark.

'Wait here, Jim,' I said. 'I'm going to go to St Petersburg. I'll try to get some news.'

I paddled quickly to the town. Then I listened through people's windows. I heard people talking.

My father had told people about my disappearance. But many people did not believe his story. 'He has killed his son,' they said. 'He wanted Huckleberry's money. Now he has murdered the boy.'

And soon, my father had disappeared too. Nobody was searching for me any longer. But there was some bad news. Miss Watson wanted to pay a reward for Jim. Many men were searching for him. And that afternoon, somebody had searched the shore, south of the town. They had seen smoke coming from Jackson's Island. It was the smoke from our fire!

4

On the Raft

I returned quickly to the island and I told Jim my news.

'We must start travelling now, Jim,' I said. 'Lots of men will come here in the morning. They'll bring dogs with them and the dogs will find us easily. We must leave the island now!'

'We'll go to Cairo on the raft, Huck,' said Jim. 'We'll sell the raft there. We'll buy tickets for the Ohio River steamboat with the money. I don't want to be a slave any longer!'

We got the raft from its hiding place. We put our clothes and our food in the little hut on the raft. And one hour after my return to the island, we steered the raft out into the current. Soon, the great Mississippi River was taking us away from St Petersburg.

We travelled every night. Nobody could see us in the dark. Then each day, we steered the raft to the shore and hid it under the trees and bushes. Jim was in great danger in the daylight. Missouri was a slave state, it wasn't a free state. And in Illinois, people captured runaway slaves. Then they took the slaves back to their owners and they got rewards.

'I'm frightened, Huck,' Jim said. 'The white men will capture me here. They'll sell me to a slave trader. Or they'll take me back to Miss Watson and get the reward. I'm not safe here!'

Jim was right. He didn't have any legal papers. He couldn't say, 'I'm not a slave any longer. My owner gave me my freedom.' Free black men had legal papers.

'Miss Watson will put a notice in the newspapers,' Jim said. 'There will be a picture of me and news about the reward. White men from the towns near the river will search for me.'

We were very careful during the day. But each evening, I went alone into a small town or a village. I bought some food. I used the money from the little floating house. And each night, Jim and I steered the raft down the river. I steered for four hours and Jim slept for four hours. Then Jim steered and I slept.

On the fifth night of our journey, we travelled past the bright lights of a great city. I was steering the raft with the long pole. I didn't wake Jim. But the next morning, I told him about the city.

'We passed St Louis last night, Jim,' I said.

Jim thought for a moment. He looked at the muddy, brown water of the Mississippi River.

'We'll get to Cairo in about seven days from now,' he said. 'Soon, I'll be a free man. You're a good boy, Huck. You've helped your friend. I'll never forget that.'

There were tears in Jim's eyes. He was happy. But I was worried. Was I doing the right thing? Jim was Miss Watson's property. Was I stealing him from her? I was poor, but I was a white person. I was helping a black slave. I was breaking the law. I thought about it for a while. But I liked Jim. He had always been kind to me. I liked him better than my father. I liked him better than most white people. I was breaking the law, but I didn't care.

Later that morning, Jim asked me a question.

'Why does the city have the name "St Louis", Huck?' he asked. 'Who was St Louis?'

'St Louis was a king of France, a long time ago, Jim,' I said.

'We don't have a king in America, Huck,' Jim said.

'No, Jim,' I said. 'The countries in Europe have kings and princes and dukes. We don't have them in America. They're old-fashioned ideas. We have different ideas in America now. Mrs Douglas sent me to the school in St Petersburg. I learnt about kings and princes and dukes there. Seventy years ago, the King of England was our king too. But we don't have a king now. America has a president now. Presidents are much better than kings.'

'Do people own slaves in Europe, Huck?' Jim asked.

I thought for a moment.

'No, Jim, people don't have slaves in Europe any longer,' I said. 'Black people have freedom there.'

'I understand you, Huck,' said Jim. 'Freedom is an old-fashioned idea!'

Five nights later, there was thick fog on the river. We couldn't see any lights on the shore. We had to travel at night, but we couldn't steer the raft easily.

There was thick fog for three days. Jim was worried. On the third day he told me the reason.

'We mustn't pass Cairo, Huck,' he said. 'The town will be quiet at night. We must look for the lights of the town on the eastern shore.'

But the next morning, the fog began to disappear. Daylight came and we steered the raft to the eastern shore of the river. Suddenly, Jim pointed at the water. The water in the middle of the river had been brown and muddy. But the water near the shore was not brown and muddy, it was clear and bright.

'Oh, Huck,' Jim said. 'We've come too far. We passed Cairo in the night. This clear, bright water comes from the Ohio River!'

5

Decisions

'What shall we do, Huck?' Jim asked.

'I must try to buy a little boat, Jim,' I said. 'We can't move this big raft back up the river. But I can paddle a small boat up the river. You must hide in the hut on the raft now. I'll find the nearest village. I'll talk to people there. Somebody will sell me a small boat. Then you must hide in the bottom of the boat. I'll cover you with clothes. I'll paddle the boat back to Cairo.'

Jim hid in the hut and I started to move the raft out into the current again. But after a moment, I heard somebody shouting to me. I looked round.

Two white men were paddling a boat towards us. They stopped their boat near the raft. One of them spoke to me.

'Have you seen any black men here, boy?' he said. 'Five slaves have escaped from a farm near here. There's a reward for them.'

'No,' I said. 'I haven't seen any black men.'

'Are there *any* men in the hut on your raft?' he asked.

'There's – there's one man, sir,' I answered. 'My father is in there.'

The man didn't believe me.

'Your father?' he said. 'We'll come onto your raft and look in the hut, boy. We'll talk to your father!'

I was frightened. The men were going to find Jim! I didn't want any trouble. Jim *was* a runaway slave. I thought for a moment. Then I made a decision. I started to cry loudly.

'Yes, please come onto the raft,' I said. 'My father is very sick. I'm very worried about him. He has red marks all over his body. I must find a doctor for him.'

'No, we won't come onto your raft now,' the man said quickly. 'We believe your story. But stay away from us, boy! You'll find a doctor in the next town on the eastern shore. It's twenty miles south of here.'

The man threw some money onto the raft.

'There's $40,' he said. 'Pay the doctor with it. Buy some food in the next town. But start travelling *now!*'

The men paddled away very quickly. I steered the raft into the current. I heard Jim laughing quietly inside the hut.

A mile further on, I steered the raft to the shore again. We hid it under some bushes. Then Jim and I sat in the hut and we talked. Later, we ate some food and we went to sleep for a few hours.

In the afternoon, we were awake again. Suddenly, we heard a lot of noise in the bushes near the river. People were running through the bushes and shouting. We heard some dogs barking too. I understood these noises. Some men with dogs were hunting somebody or something.

'Are those men hunting the five runaway slaves?' I asked myself.

A moment later, I knew the answer to my question. Two men ran out of the bushes near the shore. The two men saw the raft and they jumped onto it.

The two men weren't slaves, they were white men. But they were running away from somebody! Quickly, they hid in the little hut with Jim.

'Please hide us,' they said. 'Those men want to kill us. Please move your raft out into the current. We must get away from this place!'

These men were runaways. What had they done? I didn't know. But Jim and I were runaways too. I made another decision.

'All right,' I said. 'We'll help you!'

6

The King and the Duke

Soon it was dark, and the raft was floating quickly down the river again. I looked at our visitors. One of the men was about sixty years old. He was ugly and bald. The other was about thirty. He was tall and handsome.

'Who are you?' I asked them. 'Why were those men hunting you?'

The old man spoke first.

'I've had a very hard life,' he said. 'I am not an American. I am the King of France.'

I looked at him carefully. His clothes were old and dirty.

'I left France when I was a young man,' he said. 'The French people had a revolution. They killed my father.'

'You speak English well, King,' I said.

'Yes,' he replied. I had to leave France quickly. I was young then. I've forgotten the French language. I can't speak it now. I came to this country a long time ago. Now, I travel from town to town. I tell people about God. I tell them about my life. But one day, the French people will want me again. Then I'll return to my own country. One day, I'll be the King in Paris.'

I looked at the younger man.

'Are you a Frenchman too?' I asked him.

'No,' he replied. 'I'm an Englishman. I'm a duke. I'm the Duke of Bridgewater.'

'Did you have to leave *your* country too?' I asked him.

'Yes,' he said. 'Some wicked people stole my money and my land. Now I live in your country and I work here. I was a printer for many years. I worked for a newspaper. But now I'm an actor. I act parts of William Shakespeare's plays. I act in the towns and villages by the river. I try to give these simple people something beautiful! But sometimes they try to attack me. Why? I don't know the answer.'

Soon, the two men wanted to sleep.

'I am a king,' the older man said. 'I must sleep in the hut.'

'And I am a duke,' the younger man said. 'I must sleep in the hut too.'

I wasn't happy about this. But Jim agreed with our visitors. Jim and I had to sleep outside the hut. It was cold.

'Kings from France and dukes from England are fine people, Huck,' Jim said. 'There aren't any slaves in their countries.'

I didn't say anything. I knew the truth. The older man wasn't a king, and he wasn't a Frenchman. The younger man wasn't a duke, and he wasn't an Englishman. I knew that. They were both Americans. They were confidence tricksters. They told lies to people and they tricked people. They wanted people to give them money. But I didn't want to tell Jim about that. He trusted our visitors. He was a good man and he always believed people's stories.

The two confidence tricksters were criminals. And they were runaways. But I didn't care about that. Jim and I were runaways too.

The next morning, the King and the Duke started asking me questions about Jim.

'Is he a runaway slave?' they asked.

I thought for a moment. Missouri and Illinois were behind us. The state of Arkansas was on the western shore of the river, and the state of Tennessee was on the eastern shore. But these were slave states too. I didn't trust our visitors. Did they want to sell Jim? Did they want to send him back to Miss Watson? Did they want the reward? I didn't know. But I didn't trust them!

'We must be very careful,' I thought. I didn't tell them the truth about Jim. I talked about something different. But soon, the two confidence tricksters wanted the answer to another question.

'You don't travel in the daylight,' the Duke said. 'Why not?'

'I'm worried about Jim,' I replied. 'I don't want anybody to see him. The people here don't know about free black men. They say, "All black men are slaves." They'll try to capture him. They'll try to sell him.'

Later that morning, the King and the Duke walked to a small town near the river. I went with them, but Jim stayed on the raft.

There was nobody in the town. That was very strange! But we saw a notice on the wall of a shop. And then we understood. Everybody had gone to a religious meeting in a big tent, half a mile away.

We went to the office of the town's newspaper. The Duke of Bridgewater looked carefully through the windows. There was nobody inside.

'You must go with the King, Huck,' he said to me. 'I'm going to use the newspaper's printing machine.'

The Duke went into the office. And I went with the King of France to the religious meeting in the big tent.

Inside the tent, the minister was telling everybody about God. He shouted and he hit the table with his hand.

'God loves all of you!' the minister shouted. 'God loves good people. And he loves bad people too. But bad people must repent of their sins.'

Some of the people in the tent shouted, 'Yes!'

'Bad people must tell God about their sins,' the minister said. 'And they must tell their friends and their neighbours about their sins. They must repent of their sins. They must say, "I'm sorry!" They must say it to God, and they must say it to their friends and neighbours!'

'Yes!' the people shouted again.

Suddenly the King of France held up his arms.

'What are you doing?' I asked him.

'I'm going to repent of my sins,' he said quietly. 'We can get some money from these good people!'

The King walked up to the minister.

'I have been a bad man,' he said. 'I was a pirate in the South Seas. My men and I stole gold from people. I came here to America with lots of money. But I spent all the money. Now I have no money.'

The King turned to all the people in the tent.

'God took my money from me!' he shouted. 'I know that now. God wanted me to repent of my sins.'

'Yes!' shouted the people.

'This morning, I made a decision,' said the King of France. 'I said to myself, "Tomorrow, I will go back to the South Seas. I will go back to my men. We will steal some more gold." But then I came here, to this meeting. God sent me here, my friends. Now I want to repent of my sins!'

'Yes!' shouted the people.

'I have no money,' said the King. 'But today, I have a plan. I want to go back to the South Seas. I want to tell my men about God. I want to tell them about his love. I want my men to repent of their sins.'

A moment later, the minister was walking round the tent. People were giving him money. Soon, he had $87. He gave the money to the King.

'God will help you, dear brother,' he said.

'Yes!' the people shouted.

'Take God's love with you to the pirates of the South Seas!' the minister said.

'Yes!' the people shouted again.

We went back to the raft. The King had $87 and he was very happy. The Duke was waiting for us at the raft. He showed us a large sheet of paper. There were some words and a big picture on it. It was a reward notice. The Duke had printed the notice at the newspaper office.

7

The Confidence Tricksters

I asked the Duke about the reward notice for Jim.

'Why did you print that notice?' I asked.

'We want to travel in the daylight, Huck,' he replied. 'We'll fix the notice to the hut on the raft. And we'll tie Jim to the raft with a rope. People will see Jim and they'll see the notice. They'll say, "These good white men have captured a runaway slave. They are taking him back to his owner in New Orleans." After that, nobody will stop us.'

Jim wasn't happy about this plan. He didn't want to be tied to the raft all day. But I agreed with the Duke's idea.

We did not move the raft that night. The next morning, we tied Jim with the rope and we moved out into the current again.

Two days later, we came to a big town by the river. We stopped the raft there. There was a meeting room in the town. Two hundred people could sit in this room. The Duke wanted to use the room that evening.

'Two hundred people can sit in this room,' he said.

The Duke found the owner of the meeting room and he paid some money to the man. Then the Duke showed us some notices. He had printed them at the newspaper office. We fixed them on the buildings in the town.

TONIGHT AT NINE O'CLOCK

THERE WILL BE

AN EXCITING PERFORMANCE

IN THE TOWN MEETING ROOM

THIS PERFORMANCE IS ONLY FOR MEN OVER 21 YEARS OLD!

PRICE: ONE DOLLAR!

The Duke had printed these notices at the newspaper office too. But they weren't reward notices.

'We must travel tonight,' the Duke said. 'We must be ready at nine o'clock.'

'But the performance in the town meeting room will happen at nine o'clock,' I said.

The Duke did not answer me, but he smiled.

That evening, the King of France and I stood near the door of the town meeting room. About two hundred men were standing in a line. They all wanted to come in. Most of them were wearing hats and scarves. Their scarves covered the lower parts of their faces. Their hats covered the upper parts of their faces. But we could see their eyes! Their eyes were bright!

Each of the men gave the King a dollar. Then they sat down inside the room. At nine o'clock, the Duke walked to the front of the room.

'Gentlemen, the performance will start in two minutes!' he said. 'And now we must turn off all the lights!'

A few moments later, the big room was dark. The excited men were waiting for the performance. But the King, the Duke and I were running towards the raft. We jumped onto the raft and I steered it away from the shore.

After five minutes, there was a loud noise behind us in the town. Two hundred angry men were shouting.

We travelled all that night and all the next day. The King wanted to travel a long way from that town!

'We had to pay ten dollars for the room,' said the Duke. 'But we took $205 dollars from those people!'

One morning, we came to a small town on the eastern shore. There was a pier for boats there. Big steamboats stopped at the pier. Passengers got onto the boats there and they got off the boats there. We tied Jim with his rope. Then we jumped off the raft and we climbed up onto the pier.

A young man was standing on the pier.

He saw us and he walked over to the King of France and the Duke of Bridgewater.

'My name is Tom Collins,' he said. 'Are you two gentlemen the brothers of Peter Wilks? Are you Mr Harvey Wilks, sir?' he asked the King. 'And is this your brother, Mr William Wilks?'

The King didn't say no. He looked at the man for a moment, then he spoke sadly.

'Have you some news for us?' he asked.

'Yes, sir,' the young man replied. 'It's bad news. Peter Wilks died yesterday. He freed his slaves in the morning, and he died in the afternoon. His funeral will happen tomorrow. He was a good man.'

'Yes, he was a good man!' the King said. 'Tell us about our brother Peter's life here, in this fine town.'

The King was a very clever man. Soon we had heard the story of Peter Wilks' life.

Peter Wilks had been an Englishman. He had come to America many years before. He had come to this small town. He had married an American woman, and they had had three daughters. Peter Wilks had two brothers, Harvey and William, but they had stayed in England. Harvey was a minister. William was deaf and dumb – he couldn't hear and he couldn't speak.

A few weeks before, Peter Wilks had become very ill. Soon, he was dying. He had written to his brothers in England. He wanted them to come to America. His wife was dead. He wanted his brothers to take care of his daughters.

Tom Collins finished his story. 'Peter wanted his brothers to have his money, after his death,' he said.

Suddenly, the King smiled sadly.

Thank you for this news, young man,' the King said. 'Yes! I *am* Harvey Wilks. This is my brother, William.' He pointed at the Duke. Then he pointed at me. 'And this is our servant, Huckleberry.'

I smiled at Mr Collins, but I didn't speak.

'We didn't get here before Peter's death,' the King said. 'That's sad! We'll go to his house now.'

Tom Collins pointed to Peter Wilks' house. Then he got onto a steamboat. Soon, he had gone.

Many of Peter Wilks' neighbours were in the sitting room of his house. And Peter's three daughters were there too. The oldest girl, Mary Jane, was nineteen. Susan was fifteen and Joanna was fourteen.

The King tried to speak with an English voice. It was a strange voice. Was that how Englishmen spoke? I didn't know! The Duke didn't speak. He didn't have to speak. He had to be deaf and dumb!

'I am your Uncle Harvey,' the King said to the girls. 'I'm a minister.' Then he pointed at the Duke. 'And this is your Uncle William,' he said. 'He can't speak. But I am speaking for him.'

'And who is this?' Mary Jane asked. She pointed at me.

'This is our servant, Huckleberry,' the King replied. 'He is an American,' the King said. 'But he's been my servant for many years. We will all stay here for a few days.'

Peter Wilks' body was in a big wooden coffin in the dining room of the house. The girls took us into the room. The coffin was open. Its lid was next to the door, against the wall. We all looked inside the coffin.

'Goodbye, my dear brother,' the King said to Peter Wilks' body. There were tears in the King's eyes. And there were tears in the Duke's eyes too.

We went back to the sitting room. Then Mary Jane left the room. A minute later, she came back with a heavy bag. She gave it to the King.

'You are going to take care of us now, Uncle,' she said. 'Here is Father's money. There is $6000 in this bag. Father wanted you to have it.'

I looked at Mary Jane. She had beautiful red hair. I liked her very much. I began to worry about the King's plan. Mary Jane trusted us. I didn't want to trick her. But I didn't say anything then.

8

The Coffin

In the afternoon, some more neighbours came to the house. All the men drank wine and they talked about Peter Wilks.

One of the neighbours was the town's doctor.

The King was talking about his dead brother, Peter. And he was talking about God. The doctor listened to him carefully. Suddenly, he spoke angrily.

'Sir, you know nothing about God!' the doctor said. 'You are not a minister! And you are not an Englishman. Your voice is not an English voice. You are an American. You are not Peter Wilks' brother, Harvey. You are a confidence trickster!'

Peter's friends and neighbours heard the doctor's words. They were surprised. But they didn't believe the doctor. And Peter's daughters didn't believe him.

'He *is* father's brother!' Mary Jane said to the doctor. 'He knows everything about Father's life.'

This was true! Tom Collins had told the King everything about Peter Wilks' life.

The doctor was angry, and he left the house.

That night, the King and the Duke went to their bedroom early. They took the bag of money with them. I went to my bedroom too. I got into the bed, but I couldn't sleep. I was thinking about the two tricksters.

'I won't help them,' I thought. 'They want to take $6000 from these girls. The girls will have nothing. They'll have to leave their home. What shall I do?'

I thought for a while. Then I had an idea.

'I'll take the bag of money and I'll hide it,' I thought. 'The King and the Duke won't find it. Soon, we'll leave this town. Then I'll write a letter to Mary Jane. I'll tell her about the hiding place.'

This was a good plan. I didn't want any trouble with judges or lawyers. And I didn't want any white men to capture Jim. But I did want Mary Jane to have her father's money.

I got out of bed and I went quietly to the tricksters' bedroom. The King and the Duke had drunk a lot of wine. They did not wake.

After a few moments, I found the bag of money in a

cupboard. Quickly, I left the room with it.

'Where shall I hide the money?' I asked myself. 'Shall I bury it in the ground?'

I went down the stairs. But suddenly I heard a noise. Somebody was coming down the stairs behind me.

I ran into the dining room. I looked around the room for a hiding place. There wasn't a hiding place for me, but there was a hiding place for the money. I hid the bag in the coffin, under Peter Wilks' body!

A moment later, Mary Jane came into the room.

'What are you doing here, Huckleberry?' she asked me.

'I couldn't sleep,' I replied. 'But I'm going back to bed now. Goodnight, Miss Mary Jane.'

I went back to my bedroom.

'I'll get up again later,' I said to myself. 'I'll find another hiding place for the money.'

But I was very tired. Soon, I was asleep.

I woke up late the next morning. I went downstairs quickly and I went into the dining room.

Somebody had put the lid on the coffin! They had fixed the lid with big screws. I couldn't move it.

'Oh, no!' I said to myself. 'What am I going to do now?'

I went to the sitting room. Mary Jane was there. I talked to her, but I didn't tell her about the money.

A few minutes later, the King and the Duke came downstairs. They were angry.

'Someone has stolen the bag of money,' the King said to me. He spoke quietly. 'Do you know anything about it?'

'No,' I said. 'I don't know anything about it. But Peter Wilks freed his slaves before his death. Mr Collins told us that. The slaves left the house this morning. They got on the steamboat and they went south. Mary Jane told me that. Did they take the money?'

‘Yes! The slaves have taken it! They’ve tricked us!’ the King said angrily.

The King said a lot of things about the slaves. He said a lot of things about *all* slaves. He said a lot of very bad words! The King and the Duke were tricksters, but they hated other tricksters.

‘We musn’t say anything about this to the Wilks family!’ the Duke said. ‘We’ll think of a plan later. We must all go to the funeral now.’

Soon, we were at the town’s graveyard. We were standing round a deep grave. All Peter Wilks’ friends and neighbours were there. The three girls were crying.

The town's minister said some prayers. And the King said some prayers too. We watched six strong men putting the coffin into the grave. Then we went back to the house and we started eating and drinking.

I was unhappy. I was worried about the three girls.

'The King and the Duke won't stay here now,' I thought. 'We'll go back to the raft tonight. In a few days, we'll be a long way from here. Then I'll write to Mary Jane. I'll write, "Your father's money is with him in the coffin." She'll tell her neighbours about it. They'll dig up the coffin from the grave. Then the girls will have their father's money again.'

9

More Brothers!

Soon there was another problem. Two men came to the house that afternoon. One of them was about sixty years old. The other man was younger.

'We have come from England,' the older man said sadly. 'I am Harvey Wilks, and this is my brother William. He can't speak and he can't hear. He is deaf and dumb. I got Peter's letter. We started travelling immediately. Is my brother dead?'

The girls were angry with these men. Peter Wilks' friends and neighbours were angry too.

'You are confidence tricksters,' one of the neighbours said. 'Peter's brothers are here!' She pointed at the King and the Duke.

The two men looked at the King and the Duke.

'No!' said the older man. 'We are Peter's brothers. *These* men are confidence tricksters.'

Soon the two Harvey Wilkses were shouting at each other angrily.

The three girls and most of Peter's friends and neighbours believed the King. But a few people believed the other man. Then somebody remembered the doctor. The doctor had not believed the King. The doctor was a clever man. The neighbours wanted him to talk to the second Harvey Wilks.

Somebody ran to the doctor's house. They brought

him back to Peter's sitting room.

The doctor listened to the second Harvey Wilks. But he didn't believe the man's story. He didn't believe him, and he didn't believe the King!

'You are *all* confidence tricksters!' he said.

Soon, people were shouting at each other again. Everybody was angry.

'Be quiet!' the doctor shouted. 'I have a question for these two men.' He pointed at the King and at the other Harvey Wilks.

'I knew Peter very well,' the doctor said. 'I was his doctor for many years. There was a brown mark on Peter's body. He was born with the mark. It was on his body all his life. Both these men say, "Peter was my brother." Peter's brother must know about the mark!'

'Where was the mark on Peter's body?' he asked the two Harvey Wilkses.

'The mark was on his left leg,' said the King.

'No! It was on his right arm,' said the other man.

'They are both wrong!' the doctor said.

Soon everybody was shouting again. And soon one of Peter's friends had an idea.

'We'll go to the graveyard now and we'll dig up the coffin,' he said. 'We'll look at Peter's body. We'll find the brown mark on his leg or his arm!'

A few minutes later, we were all standing round the grave again.

'There's going to be trouble,' the King said quietly to the Duke and me. 'We'll have to run!'

Soon, there was a big crowd of people round the grave. Everybody in the town had heard the story about Peter Wilks' brothers. The neighbours had dug up the coffin from the grave. They were taking the screws out of the lid. The King and the Duke and I moved quietly to the edge of the crowd of people.

Then, somebody found the bag of money in Peter's coffin. And the King, the Duke and I started running.

A few minutes later, we jumped onto the raft and we moved out into the current. We travelled all night and all the next day.

Two days later, we stopped at another town. It was a small town on the western shore. We were in the state of Arkansas. And the King did a terrible thing there. He sold Jim!

The Duke and I went into the town that morning. The Duke wanted to find a meeting room. The King didn't come with us.

'We lost $6000 at Peter Wilks' house,' he said. 'We need some more money. We'll have another "Exciting Performance For Men Over Twenty-one" here tonight.' He laughed.

We found a meeting room and the Duke paid some money to the owner. Then he left me. He was going to find the King.

I walked slowly back to the raft. Everything was very quiet. Why? I jumped onto the raft and I looked in the little hut. Jim wasn't there. And the reward notice wasn't on the raft!

'Oh, no!' I thought. 'Somebody has captured Jim.'

I quickly moved the raft to another place, a mile away. Then I went back into the town. Soon, I found the Duke, and I told him about Jim.

'I know about Jim,' the Duke said. 'The King sold him this morning. He sold him to a farmer. The farmer's name is Phelps. His farm is five miles away.'

'The King showed Mr Phelps the reward notice,' said the Duke. 'The King said, "I don't want to go to New Orleans with this runaway. I have to go to St Louis. Give me $50 for the runaway slave. Then take him to his owner. You'll get the reward of $200." Mr Phelps agreed with the plan. He's taken Jim to his farm. He'll take him down the river to New Orleans tomorrow.'

I walked sadly away. I didn't tell the Duke where the raft was. I didn't want to see him again. Soon, I was talking to the owner of the town's store. I asked him about the road to Mr Phelps' farm. Then I told the man about the King and the Duke. I told him about the 'Exciting Performance For Men Over Twenty-one'.

Half an hour later, I walked out of the town, towards Mr Phelps' farm. Behind me, I heard a lot of angry people shouting. I smiled.

I got to Mr Phelps' farm two hours later. I didn't see anybody near the farmhouse. But I did see a wooden hut with a strong lock on the door.

10

Tom Sawyer

'Is Jim in that hut?' I asked myself.

I walked up to the hut and I called quietly through the door.

'Jim? Are you there?' I said.

'Huck!' said Jim's voice from inside the hut. 'Is that you, Huck?'

'Don't worry, Jim,' I said. 'I'll soon get you out of there.'

I said those words. I wanted Jim to be happy. But I didn't have a plan. What was I going to do?

At that moment, the door of the farmhouse opened. A large, pretty woman was standing in the doorway.

'Tom!' she said. 'You're Tom Sawyer from St Petersburg! I've been waiting for you. I'm your Aunt Polly's cousin, Sally Phelps. Polly told me about your visit. I've never seen you before, but your aunt has told me everything about you. And you've come at last, boy. Good! I'm happy! You must call me "Aunt Sally". My husband isn't at home now. But he'll be back later. And he'll be happy too!'

I was lucky! I smiled at the large woman.

'I'll be Tom Sawyer for a few days,' I said to myself. 'I know about Tom's family. I can answer questions about them. I'll stay here for a few days.'

I wanted to stay at the farm. I wanted to help Jim. I had

to think of a plan. I started to speak.

'Yes,' I said. 'I'm Tom.'

But at that moment, I heard a voice behind me.

'Huck! What are you doing here?' somebody shouted. It was a boy's voice. And I knew that voice. It was Tom Sawyer!

I told Tom about my adventures on the Mississippi River. Tom and his Aunt Sally listened to my story and they laughed.

Then Tom told us some good news.

'You left St Petersburg with Jim,' Tom said. 'But soon after that, Miss Watson died. She had tried to sell Jim, but she was very sorry about that. She wasn't a bad person. Before her death, she freed Jim. Jim isn't a slave any longer!'

Soon, we brought Jim from the wooden hut. Aunt Sally gave him some food.

'What are you going to do now, Huck?' Tom asked me.

'I don't want to go back to St Petersburg,' I said. 'I'm afraid of my father. He'll kill me one day.'

'Huck,' said Jim sadly. 'I must tell you something. Do you remember that floating house in the river? We saw it near Jackson's Island. There was a dead man inside it. Somebody had shot him. I didn't let you see the dead man. He was your father, Huck. I didn't tell you then. I didn't want you to be unhappy.'

'You're a good man, Jim,' I said quietly. 'But I'm not

unhappy.'

Then Aunt Sally spoke.

'You must stay here with us now, Huck,' she said. 'You'll wear clean clothes. You'll wash your face every day. You'll sleep in a soft bed every night. You'll be happy here!'

That happened yesterday. Tomorrow morning, I'm going to start travelling again!

Macmillan Education Limited
4 Crinan Street
London N1 9XW

Companies and representatives throughout the world

Macmillan Readers Beginner Adventures of Huckleberry Finn, The
ISBN: 978-1-035-16592-6
Macmillan Readers Beginner Adventures of Huckleberry Finn, The with eBook and Resources
ISBN: 978-1-035-16595-7

This is a retold version by F. H. Cornish of the original work by Mark Twain.

First published 2000
This edition published 2025

Illustrated by Paul Fisher Johnson
Cover photograph by Getty/Hulton Archive/George Pickow/Stringer
Photograph on page 4 by Alamy/Universal Art Archive

Printed and bound in Brazil
2025
3